THE UNOFFICIAL *FORTNITE*®
SURVIVAL GUIDE

PERFECTING YOUR DANCE MOVES IN *FORTNITE*®

TRACY BROWN HAMILTON

I0808705

Enslow Publishing
101 W. 23rd Street
Suite 240
New York, NY 10011
USA
enslow.com

As always, for Caroline Bourgeout

Published in 2020 by Enslow Publishing, LLC
101 W. 23rd Street, Suite 240, New York, NY 10011

Library of Congress Cataloging-in-Publication Data

Names: Stern, Ray.
Title: Perfecting your dance moves in Fortnite® / Ray Stern.
Description: New York : Enslow Publishing, 2020. | Series: The unofficial Fortnite® survival guide | Includes glossary and index.
Identifiers: ISBN 9781978517233 (pbk.) | ISBN 9781978517257 (library bound) | ISBN 9781978517240 (6 pack)
Subjects: LCSH: Fortnite Battle Royale (Game)--Juvenile literature. | Imaginary wars and battles--Juvenile literature. | Video games--Juvenile literature.
Classification: LCC GV1469.35.F67 S874 2020 | DDC 794.8--dc23

Printed in the United States of America

CONTENTS

INTRODUCTION

Fortnite is one of the most popular online games of recent years. Since its first release in 2017 by Epic Games, the online multiplayer game has become a worldwide sensation. Existing in three separate modes: *Fortnite*: Save the World, in which up to four players battle for survival, defending themselves from creatures and protecting objects with forts; *Fortnite*: Battle Royale, in which up to one hundred players battle to be the last surviving player; and *Fortnite* Creative, in which players can use their own imagination to develop online worlds and battles. By November 2018, *Fortnite*: Battle Royale had more than two hundred million registered users globally, according to the Statistics Panel.

Although the game is primarily a survival-shooter game, the engaging game requires players to apply a vast range of skills. A player is dropped on an island and tasked with discovering survival tools such as resources and weapons, navigating the game's island setting, working together and fairly with other players,

Players guide their characters through the island settings of *Fortnite*, battling each other for Victory Royale.

and encouraging social interaction. Positive gameplay is key as players battle for survival.

But another interesting phenomenon has arisen from the virtual battlefield: the role of dance in the game, which adds a level of strategy, fun, and, more recently, controversy, as some entertainers have planned lawsuits against Epic Games, claiming they do not own the legal right to use certain dances in the game.

The following text focuses on the dance feature of all modes of *Fortnite*, emphasizing how dance is used strategically, how to discover areas where dancing is permitted, the origins of the *Fortnite* dances, and even how to create your own custom dance moves to use during play. It also focuses on the positive impact of dance during play—both for keeping players moving and healthy but also to add a degree of fun and creativity through quirky dance moves.

CHAPTER 1

Dancing Around *Fortnite*

The dancing ability of characters during *Fortnite* play is one of the most popular features of the game. It not only adds a comedic and light touch to a game otherwise focused on shooting at enemies, but also allows players to give their characters—or avatars—a sense of individualized style and personality.

Players can dance to celebrate a big victory or simply to express themselves. Nelson Le, an avid *Fortnite* player and University of Maryland computer science major, told the *Washington Post* that while dancing adds no advantage to a player, it does add a lot of fun. Le says he often gets his characters to perform a dance while in "the lobby," the space where avatars hang out before the game actually starts. It's an entertaining, lighthearted aspect of the game that has taken the world by storm.

Players often engage in a so-called "dance-off," a feature of the game that makes it both unique and fun to play.

How to Bust a Move on Every Platform

Dances in *Fortnite* must be accessed for each player, either by purchasing them or earning them while you play. A player can have one or several dances for his or her character. *Fortnite* games, all modes, can be played on multiple platforms, or devices, and each platform has its own method of unleashing a player's ability to dance. If you are eager to join in the fun of dancing while battling for survival, you have to know how to enable the feature as you play.

So if you want to take part in this fun and physical aspect of the game and enjoy the thrill of dancing to celebrate a victory or just having a fun moment during a potentially tense and challenging game, here's how you do it:

If you are playing on PS4 or Xbox: Press the Down button on your controller as you play. You will see an option wheel that enables you to the select the emote—or dance—that you want to perform.

If you are playing on a PC and with a keyboard: Press B, which enables you to choose your emote. Do so by moving the right analog stick and press X/A, or, alternatively, move your PC's mouse. You can then select which emote you want to use by moving the right analog stick and then press X/A, or you can do this by using the mouse with your PC.

If you have only one active emote for your game character, you will not be given an option to choose your dance. Instead your default dance will be performed.

THREE *FORTNITE* DANCE MOVES AND THEIR ORIGINS

Turk's dance: The medical sitcom *Scrubs* featured a character nicknamed Turk who performed this dance during an episode, and it's become a popular *Fortnite* move.

Floss dance: The so-called Floss dance was made famous by its inventor, Russell Horning, who was born in 2001. Horning built up a following for his dance moves on Instagram, and when Katy Perry asked him to dance during one of her television performances, the footage went viral. Now known as Backpack Kid, his arm-focused dance has become a popular *Fortnite* one.

Fresh dance: Stemming from the nerdy moves of Carlton, a character on the 1990s sitcom *The Fresh*

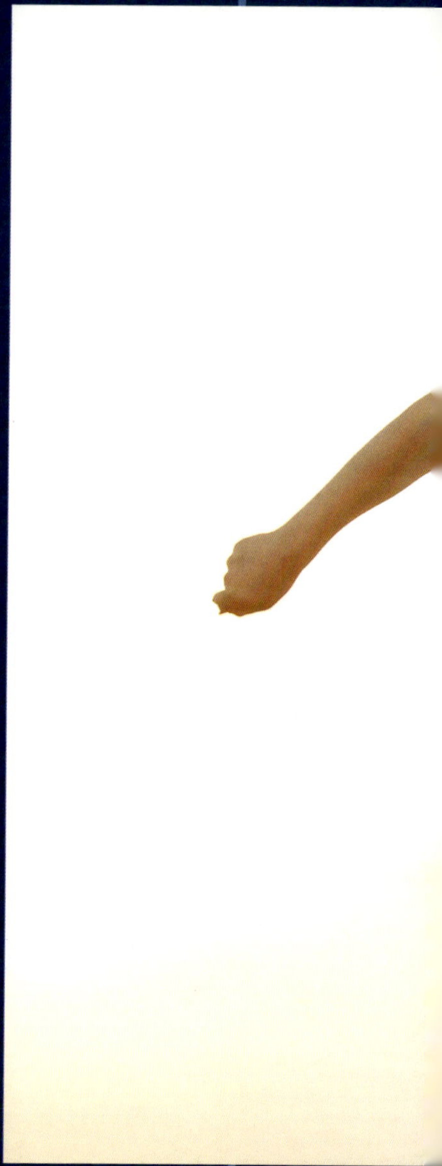

Prince of Bel-Air, Alfonso Ribeiro, the actor who played that character, popularized this dance and even performed it during his appearance on the TV show *Dancing with the Stars*.

A boy does the popular Floss dance, also called the Swish Swish dance, which was created by Russell Horning.

Interactive games like *Fortnite* are exciting, but online security should always be a concern.

Unlocking the Free Boogie Down Emote with Additional Online Security

Security is an important consideration whenever playing a game or logging into any account online. The makers of *Fortnite* are aware that their game is at risk of having users' accounts hacked. Hackers try to log in as another person and take over their account. To help players be more secure, they have offered a free emote called Boogie Down that is available to players who select "two-factor authentication" to protect their accounts.

To do this, and to have access to Boogie Down as well as extra security as your reward, go to the drop-down menu that appears beneath your name when you are logged in. Select Manage Account, and then Password and Security. Scroll down to select Two-Factor Authentication. You will receive a special code called a QR Code that you can scan using a so-called authenticator app, such as Google Authenticator. A new, temporary code will be created for you each time you attempt to log in, and any user will need both a password and this code in order to enter the account.

CHAPTER 2

Where to Dance in *Fortnite*

Dancing in *Fortnite* does not give a player more power, capability, or bring any extra advantage during play, but it does give characters the ability to gloat, express themselves, make other players laugh, and have more fun as you battle. Many characters use dancing as a means of distracting other players, but it carries no other strategic purpose.

Have This Dance

Fortnite focuses on the dancing feature of the game with weekly dance challenges, assigning players who want to join in to dance in specific locations or on specific objects, such as a sundial. The challenges require participants to not only dance in these specified spots, but, of course, to find them on the map and reach

Each player can select dance moves, which their characters can do to celebrate or taunt another character.

them safely. Polygon's online *Fortnite*: Battle Royale guide publishes weekly challenges on its site.

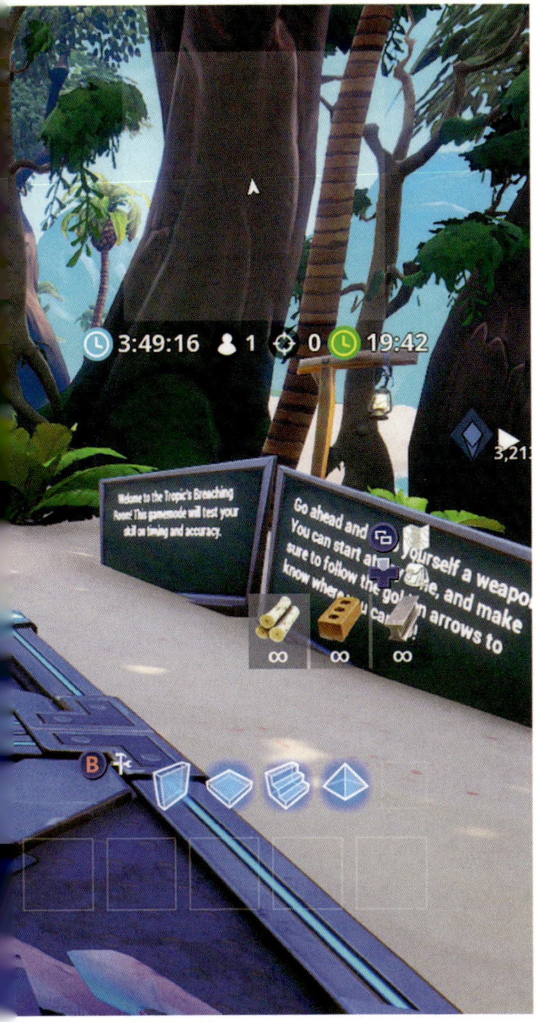

Real-life *Fortnite* dances have also become a global phenomenon. Fans of the game perform them publicly on the streets and even on television. On *The Tonight Show Starring Jimmy Fallon,* Korean pop stars BTS had a *Fortnite* dance-off. After scoring the first goal on the way to victory during the 2018 World Cup, French soccer player Antoine Griezmann performed the popular "Take the L" *Fortnite* emote. YouTube videos challenging viewers to perform *Fortnite* challenges are numerous, bringing this quirky feature of the game off the screen and into real life.

HOW TO ACCESS DANCES IN *FORTNITE*

To unlock certain dances in the game, a player must pay in V-bucks—an in-game currency that can be obtained in several ways: by being purchased with actual money, earned by advancing in the game to higher levels, helping other players, or completing daily challenges. Here are some of the most popular dances players can purchase or otherwise earn:

Infinite Dab: 500 V-Bucks

Groove Jam: Player must achieve Tier Level 95

Disco Fever: 800 V-Bucks

Swipe It: Achieve Tier Level 63

The Worm: Achieve Tier Level 28

Dance Moves: Free!

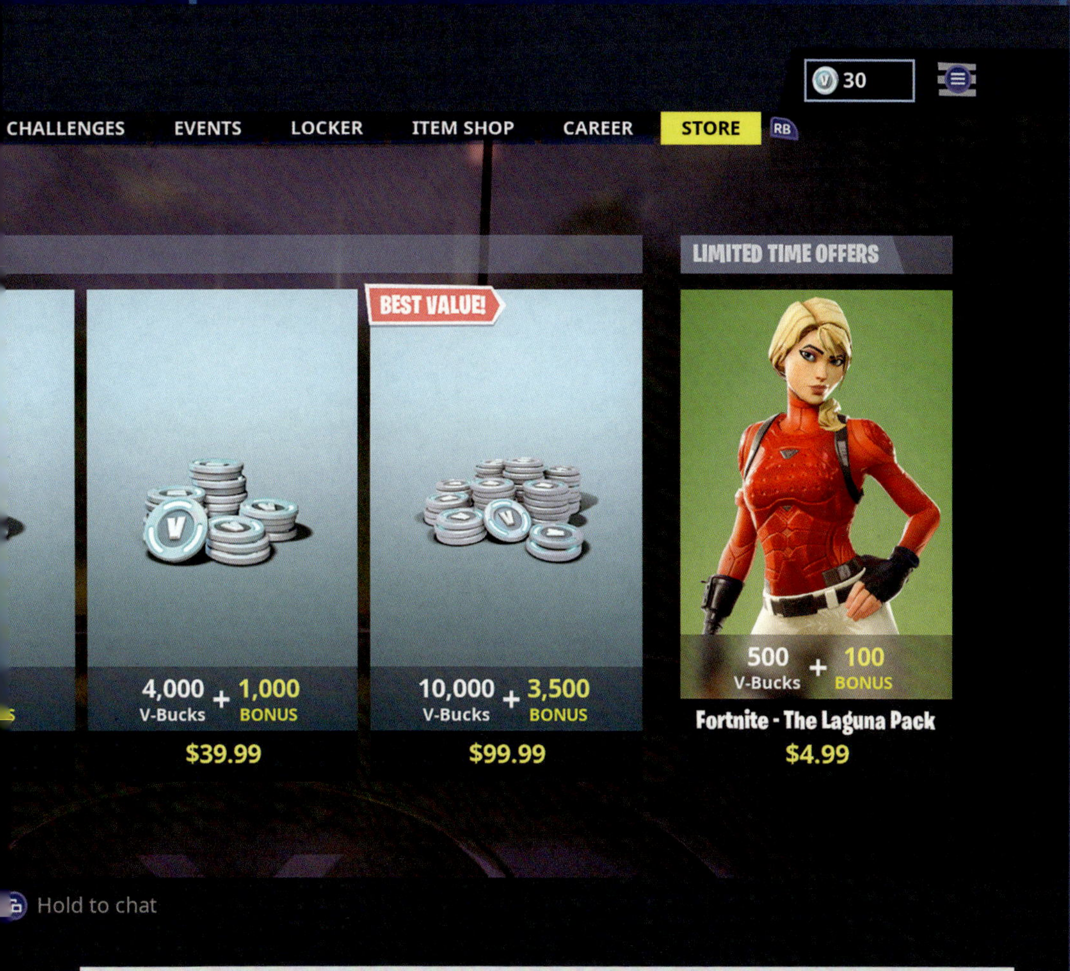

V-bucks are the in-game currency, which players acquire in various ways (including paying real money for them).

The Forbidden Dance

As popular as dancing is within *Fortnite* (and outside the game, as described in the previous section), there are places within the game where dance is expressly not allowed, although still possible. But for avid players, this just presents a new, fun challenge: how to dance where dance is forbidden. These areas are marked with No Dancing signs. The challenge to players is to find these areas and dance anyway. If you succeed, you earn five Battle Stars. Some websites, including Primagames.com, provide tips for finding these locations, although players can also discover them on their own.

Although dance is a popular feature of *Fortnite*, there are areas within the game where it is strictly forbidden.

Google "forbidden locations *Fortnite*" if you are looking for tips—but remember to always be careful when trusting information you find on the internet.

CHAPTER 3

Real-World Social Impact of *Fortnite* Dancing

Although playing video games isn't the most active pursuit all the time, the dancing aspect of *Fortnite* has kids and adults alike up and moving.

Video games are often associated with being inactive, but the dance element of *Fortnite* has gotten players up and moving.

Fitness for Fun

One benefit of *Fortnite* play is that players are moving more, learning the dances and flossing their way to fitness. In the United Kingdom, fans of *Fortnite* are paying for dance lessons in *Fortnite* fitness classes, in which participants learn various moves featured in the game, such as the Worm.

Journalist Suzanne Condie Lambert wrote in *USA Today* that her own child is dancing almost constantly due to a love of *Fortnite*. "I don't think my kid even notices he's doing it anymore," she writes. "The dance moves just happen unconsciously. Like breathing or putting the empty cereal box back on the counter instead of in the garbage." This is one outcome—intended or not—that makes playing *Fornite* a healthy and fun activity.

IS THIS DANCE LEGAL?

Although people around the world have been enjoying *Fornite* dances both onscreen and off, the game's creators have come under fire from those accusing them of copyright violations relating to some of the dances. The "inventors" of some of the dances are now claiming that Epic Games is stealing the dances without paying for the rights to mimic and use them in the game. Originators of some dances, including Alfonso Ribeiro, creator of the Carlton, known as the Fresh in *Fortnite*, believe the gaming company needs

Alfonso Ribeiro does the Carlton, a dance move he made famous on *The Fresh Prince of Bel-Air*.

to give them credit, if not money, to include their moves in the game. Chance the Rapper argued on Twitter that use of these dances is cheating, particularly of the African American artists who created many of them, writing that "Black creatives created and popularized these dances but never monetized them. Imagine the money people are spending on these Emotes being shared with the artists that made them." It's unclear how the issue will be worked out, but it has created a growing controversy.

Overall Benefits of *Fornite* Play

The game of *Fortnite* offers players a challenging quest in a social, interactive, and engaging online environment. It also emphasizes fair play and cooperation among players. The dance features takes the game to another level,

Around the world, *Fortnite* dance moves have launched a new dance and fitness craze.

allowing players to express their personalities and celebrate their victories through dance. The phenomenon has been taken to the real world, with athletes adopting certain *Fortnite*-inspired moves to celebrate a win and entertain fans. Most of all, it is encouraging players to express themselves through dancing, just like their in-game avatars do!

GLOSSARY

AVATAR A character in a video game.

BATTLE A fight between individuals or groups.

BATTLE STARS Items collected during play in order to advance your level.

COPYRIGHT Ownership of an intellectual or creative idea.

DEFEND To protect.

EMOTE A dance in *Fortnite*.

ENGAGING Something demanding someone's attention and participation.

FORT A structure designed to protect something or someone.

FORTNITE A popular online multiplayer game.

HACKER Someone who breaks into someone else's private online accounts.

INTERACTIVE Something that is social and involves communicating and working together with others.

MODE In this context, the type of *Fortnite* game being played.

ONLINE MULTIPLAYER Describing a video game that is played via a game server that allows players from all over the world to play each other.

PLATFORM In this context, a device on which a game is played.

STRATEGY A plan for achieving a goal.

SURVIVAL-SHOOTER GAME A genre of video game that tests a players strategic and reaction abilities.

TIER LEVEL A means of measuring advancement during game play.

TWITTER A social media site on which people share their opinions.

TWO-FACTOR AUTHENTICATION A method of preventing hackers with additional security.

V-BUCKS The currency used in *Fortnite* with which dances can be purchased.

VICTORY A win, a triumph.

FOR MORE INFORMATION

Dance/USA
Website: https://www.danceusa.org

High Five
Website: https://www.highfive.org

International Game Developers Association
Website: https://www.igda.org

Obesity Action Coalition
Website: https://www.obesityaction.org

Obesity Canada
Website: https://obesitycanada.ca

FOR FURTHER READING

Abbott, Josh. Fortnite *Download, Android, Mac, IOS, Xbox One, PC, Windows, APK, Unblocked, Guide Unofficial*. N.p.: Gamer Guides LLC, 2018.

Chang, Sam. *600* Fortnite *Tricks: The Expanded* Fortnite Battle Royale *Strategy Guide*. Independently published, 2018.

Cone, Theresa Purcell, and Stephen L. Cone. *Teaching Children Dance*. Champaign, IL: Human Kinetics, 2012.

Gilbert, Anne Green. *Creative Dance for All Ages*. Champaign, IL: Human Kinetics, 2015.

LeMay, Michelle, and Andrea Ambandos. *Dance Workout For Dummies*. Hoboken, NJ: Wiley, 2014.

Morgan Publishing. *How to Draw* Fortnite *for Kids and Teens: Learn to Draw All of Your Favorite Skins and Characters with This Step by Step Drawing Guide*. Nashville, TN: Morgan Publishing, 2018.

Paris, David. *History of Video Games*. Huntington Beach, CA: Teacher Created Materials, 2016.

Royston, Angela. *Ballet* (Love to Dance). Chicago, IL: Capstone, 2015.

Royston, Angela. *Hip Hop* (Love to Dance). Chicago, IL: Capstone, 2015.

Supreme Game Guides. Fortnite*: The Ultimate Guide to Dominating* Fortnite Battle Royale (*Fortnite* Guides). Independently published, 2018.

INDEX

About the Author

Tracy Brown Hamilton is a writer, editor, and journalist who has written many young adult nonfiction books on various topics, including technology, internet security, dance, and cyberbullying. She lives in the Netherlands with her husband and three children.

Photo Credits

Cover © iStockphoto.com/cheegintan; pp. 10-11 EMS-FORSTER-PRODUCTIONS/DigitalVision /Getty Images; pp. 12-13 LightField Studios/Shutterstock.com; p. 22 Clarissa Leahy/Cultura/Getty Images; p. 24 PA Images/ Alamy Stock Photo; p. 26 oneinchpunch//Shutterstock.com.

Design & Layout: Brian Garvey; Editor: Bethany Bryan;
Photo Researcher: Nicole DiMella;
Fortnite Consultant: Sam Keppeler